Strength
Of
The
Woman

Vol. 1

♥ Her Making ♥

Olivia Precious Cooper

Strength

of

The

Woman

Vol. 1

Her Making

Olivia Precious Cooper

IAP Publishing

Strength of The Woman: Her Making
Copyright © 2014 Olivia Precious Cooper
Published by IAP Publishing
A division of I Am Precious International Ministries
Email: publishing@preciousinternational.org
Website: www.preciousinternational.org
Phone: +1(615) 669-6460

Unless otherwise identified, Scripture is taking from THE HOLY
BIBLE, NEW INTERNATIONAL VERSION®, NIV® Copyright © 1973,
1978, 1984, 2011 by Biblica, Inc.™ Used by permission. All rights reserved
worldwide.

Scripture marked MSG is taken from The Message copyright © 1993,
1994, 1995, 1996, 2000, 2001, 2002. Used by permission of NavPress
Publishing Group.

Scripture marked AMP is taken from the Amplified® Bible, Copyright
© 1954, 1958, 1962, 1964, 1965, 1987 by The Lockman Foundation. Used by
permission." (www.Lockman.org)

"Scripture quotations taken from the New American Standard Bible®,
Copyright © 1960, 1962, 1963, 1968, 1971, 1972, 1973, 1975, 1977, 1995 by The
Lockman Foundation. Used by permission." (www.Lockman.org)

ISBN-10: 0983015759
ISBN-13: 978-0983015758

Printed in the United States of America

Ordering Information:

Quantity sales. Special discounts are available on quantity purchases by
ministries, associations, and others. For details, contact the publisher at the
address above.

Dedication

I dedicate this to everyone in search of The Woman as created by God Almighty. You know who you are…

I dedicate this to the women God's using as displays of His marvelous work in the earth. You know who you are…

I dedicate this to the women God used as examples and supports throughout my life. You know who you are…

I dedicate this to my mother, Aida, as a Special Thanksgiving. You know who you are.

Contents

ACKNOWLEDGMENT

For such a work, there is only one to acknowledge. He is the Second and Last Adam, the Bright and Morning Star. His Name, having no limits nor shadows, is the Name above every other name. I have bowed my heart to Him as He has named me His Own. I honor You, Jesus Christ, the One and Only begotten Son of God.

The Woman

This Book speaks of four distinct descriptions of a woman. However, our prime focus is 'The Woman'. Within the writing, you will see an interchanging relationship of her descriptions, which draws to conclusion who she really is at the end of the book. See the points below for your acquaintance with her.

- <u>The Woman or female</u> – this is the feminine characteristics of the Man creature God spoke into creation (Genesis 1:26)

- <u>Adam's woman</u> – she is the one Adam named as 'woman' meaning *bone of my bones and flesh of my flesh* (Genesis 2:23)

- <u>Eve</u> – this description is Adam's woman he renamed after the fall (Genesis 3:20)

- <u>Christ's Woman or God's Woman</u> – this is who each woman becomes once in Christ and yielded to His Spirit completely in love, revelation, obedience, and character. She is also a symbol of His Body, the Church

ENJOY YOUR READING…

~introduction

Hello!

Being that this is the first book of the series, "Strength of The Woman," let me start by saying, "This is NOT a feminist movement attempt or some women's power campaign. It is not intended to promote any women's rule world or usurp authority over the male gender in any way, shape, or form." No, this book is none of the above; and no matter your views, please do not get offended. For this book is further than what the human mind has come to comprehend on its own or will ever be able to conceive.

"Strength of The Woman" goes beyond the veil of the soulish realm, providing glimpses into the supernatural creation of God. It reveals secrets kept hidden for centuries, only to reveal them in such a time as this. I guarantee that, as you read this dynamic piece of revelation, you will receive power from whence it has come.

As always in my books, my purpose is to share Truth with my readers as God's Holy Spirit reveals it to me. One cannot fully partake of knowledge until he or she reaches maximum understanding of the subject. King Solomon said it best in Proverbs 4:7, when he stated, "The beginning of wisdom is this: Get wisdom. Though it cost all you have, get understanding."

As we gain understanding as our foundation, we will address our title and subject, which is "Strength of The Woman." That is to say, we will examine the woman first in order to know the strength she possesses. The goal is to pursue this Strength until it becomes visible in us as women.

To be a woman, you must be born as one; but to be The Woman, you must be born of the Spirit. To receive understanding of The Woman, you must be given access into the realm of God's Spirit. One might argue that it is possible to be a woman nowadays without being born one, based on the use of technology, a particular way of thinking, and the display of feminine gestures. Well, from the outward appearance that may be so, but appearances will never make that person The Woman. He may look, feel, sound, act and everything else like a woman after medical procedures and years of practice, but that will never make a male 'The Woman'.

Listen. Even a natural-born woman cannot change into the nature of The Woman until she is taken to that spiritual dimension. How much more a transvestite male? A natural born woman becomes The Woman after being born of the Spirit and that same Spirit of Truth gives birth to *that* realm of revelation. As Jesus stated in John 16:13, "…when he, the Spirit of truth, comes, he will guide you into all the truth. He will not speak on his own; he will speak only what he hears, and he will tell you what is yet to come." Because He is speaking, I ask, what is the Spirit saying concerning The Woman? What Truth does He reveal? And, what is He saying directly to The Woman?

In recent years, much has been said about women from various sources, speaking on different aspects of women. Topics include women's rights, women empowerment, women's liberation, women's health, equality, education, development, and so on. I recently had someone suggest printing T-shirts for one of our Women's Conferences with the words, "Women Empowerment." I ruled it out. Not because I am against the topic, but rather because I know it is not the way the Spirit is leading I Am Precious International Ministries.

In fact, I disliked hearing the few prophets I encountered when they prophesied to me stating that I was called to lead women and I would have a strong global women's ministry, etc. I almost hated the thought of it and somehow rejected those prophecies. Why? Well, being free-spirited, I didn't want to be stereotyped, labeled, or limited in any way. I believed that the Gospel was for everyone and that my anointing was for both sexes. So, I rebelled in my heart, but only until the Owner of the Anointing was ready for me to accomplish the work concerning women that He had called me to do. Now, here I am with a changed heart and renewed mind, but somewhere inside me a tiny voice is still yelling, "I am still not a women-only minister!" LOL.

Governments, non-governmental organizations [NGOs], and some private sectors fund projects for the development of women. Enormous amounts of resources stream monthly to address the abnormalities of issues concerning women. Can these means suffice? Being a stickler for Truth, I do not believe they can reach the root of the problems women face in general. Yet, I do bless God for everyone and every organization that has contributed and are still contributing to the well- being of women. Every effort, no matter how small, adds value to the gender, and I too have benefited from such humanitarian relief.

Notwithstanding, I ask again, what is the Spirit

saying to The Woman? Notice that I am not referring to a woman in terms of an individual, but to The Woman. What is the Spirit of God saying to The Woman? Who is The Woman? And if you haven't heard from Him as to who she is, I strongly suggest you keep reading, because God wants to reveal His Truth to you as He did to me.

Truth revealed cannot be hidden. It shines like a light elevated on a hill in the darkest of night. Everyone within distance will see its illumination. Master Jesus, in Luke 8:16–17, pronounced this Truth by saying, "No one lights a lamp and hides it in a clay jar or puts it under a bed. Instead, they put it on a stand, so that those who come in can see the light. For there is nothing hidden that will not be disclosed, and nothing concealed that will not be known or brought out into the open." Accordingly, where are you with your shine?

I am of the belief that only those with something to hide prefer to remain in the dark. They fight the very existence of light, because they are aware that light will expose their deeds, making them feel ashamed and judged. However, Jesus, the Light of the world, has come to set us free from the grips of spiritual bondage, including the darkness of ignorance. No longer should people remain in the dark, but rather, they should run to His Light to receive the freedom He brings.

Unfortunately, those shying away from Truth are

the ones perishing by the lack of knowledge, according to Hosea 4:6, and mind you, that was God speaking. Likewise, there are those who believe that, if they give the Truth they have received, they may lose their control exercised over others who remain lingering in the lack of the knowledge of God's Truth. And might I add, this form of control is a kind of witchcraft, because no one should control another person.

Here's an example of what I'm talking about. Let's say God delivered Willow from financial bondage, and now she's a church leader who is also very rich. Well, Sunflower brings her problems to Willow, seeking weekly counseling and prayer. Coincidentally, Sunflower's issues are quite similar to what God delivered Willow from, and she knows what to do to help Sunflower. But, Willow refuses to help lead her into such freedom simply because she assumes that Sunflower may no longer need her once Sunflower gains independence, which is how it should be. In addition, whom would Willow have to exercise authority over once Sunflower leaves that state of financial bondage? Now, do you see the witchcraft?

The knowledge of Truth, and not just any knowledge, is to bring people into the freedom of who they are, where they are from, where they are going, and what to do while traveling the journey with the Lord. This Truth gives freedom to live the life God designed for each person to live. It provides no room for careless living, misalignment of purpose, or the absence of restraint. Christ, Who is Truth, gives this freedom within the confinement of vision and purpose constraints.

May I suggest here that husbands should not be afraid of their wives coming into the fullness of who they are as women. Thus, I am saying that, when a woman comes to the Truth of who she is in Christ, her freedom will manifest in accordance with God's authority for her life in terms of her relationships with Creator, self, husband, children, the Church, and the world. Now, married women or soon to be married, catch the order—Creator, self, husband, children, Church, and then everything else that is permissible and expedient. With that said, I would like us to move on.

For an extreme length of time, women have suffered many abuses, assaults, prejudices, and much unfairness. But when and how did this all begin? One might insinuate that women have been undermined since the foundation of time. This then takes us back to the beginning in Garden of Eden. Oh, yes, as far back as the Garden of Eden! Could it be that imperfection existed within God's perfect Garden? Well, it's possible, depending on how we define imperfection. At this point, I ask that you familiarize yourself with Genesis, chapters 1-3, and keep it beside you as you read 'Strength of The Woman'.

Realize that, during the time of the woman appearing in the Garden of Eden, God—to some extent—stepped back to see what Adam would do. For instance, Genesis 2:19 states, "Now the LORD God had formed out of the ground all the wild animals and all the birds in the sky. He brought them to the man to see what he would name them; and whatever the man called each living creature, that was its name." This indicates that God was allowing the man to do what the man was supposed to do. In addition, naming in creation context is giving the creature the ability to express what it is named. This means that the name, which is given thus, authorizes and pronounces the nature, behaviors, limitations, boundaries, and even the future of that which receives the name.

With this pattern in play, God formed the woman and did the same. He allowed the man to name the woman, and what the man (Adam) called her is what she became. This marks the beginning of Adam's woman. For the man said, "This is now bone of my bones and flesh of my flesh; she shall be called 'woman,' for she was taken out of man." (Genesis 2:23).

Really!

After reading that one day, I got a little confused. As usual, my mind began to burn with questions concerning Adam in the naming ceremony when it got to the woman's turn. For example, are you so self-centered, Adam, that you could not see beyond self? Was that all she was to become, bone and flesh? Didn't you, Adam, know that what you call her is what she would become? Were you running low on creative descriptions after naming the animals? On the other hand, was that all you could see about her?

Ok lady, please don't applaud for those questions because they remind you of how you silently question your husband. LOL.

But, what was the scenario? What was really happening, in particular, happening to Adam when he first saw her? Now, I've heard preachers say that Adam was so wooed by the woman's appearance that all he could say was, "Wow, man." In other words, she was just too breathtaking. Is that right? How can a man be blown away by the beauty of a woman, but all he can think about is himself? You know, "...bone of my bones, flesh of my flesh...because she was taken out of [me]." Oh Adam, what happened to you in that moment? Some might define this as vanity.

I'm not male-bashing, but think about it. What was Adam really thinking when God brought The Woman? Perhaps, he truly did see an exact replica of himself. Who knows? However, could that have been the beginning of The Woman's fall? Yes, the devil is blamed for the fall but was that the opening he needed to begin his deception with her? I pray that as we travel through the series, "Strength of The Woman," you will see who she really is by understanding who she was before she met Adam. Ah, yeah, Adam!

God's design is perfection, from beginning to end. Whether things turn good or evil, His way is perfect. Which means if it is not perfect, or has fallen short in any capacity, then something or someone else other than God played a not-so-perfect role.

I hope you can think through these questions with me for deeper insights into the ways of God. What did God intend for The Woman? Was she to be the *underdog* of society? Were either of the genders to be downtrodden throughout the ages by the enemy? No. However, women in general, based on an international scale, have experienced the worst from self, men, society, the world at large, the devil, and, so sadly, religious institutions. Nevertheless, thank God for the true Body of Christ, the True Church, not the religious body naming itself after Christ.

Is there a solution to all these questions and unprecedented situations, which women have faced and to some extent, still suffer? Will we ever get to the root? Does the real Church of Jesus Christ have the solution? I say, it does, and this book is a means of revealing the Truth to set The Woman free and release her the Strength needed to live as the life Father God created her to be.

Chapter 2

~in the Beginning

Dear sister, up to this point, have you ever felt less of who you thought you should be? Alternatively, let me phrase the question like this. Have you ever felt like the "weaker vessel" in any relationship simply because you are a woman? Has it ever occurred to you that you are more than what you have told yourself and allowed others to tell you or make you feel? Frankly, do you believe that you are far greater than what and who you are right now? If so, then brace yourself for a Truth that only God can unearth. Truth buried deep under the layers of your flesh and bone.

King Solomon, in Proverbs 25:2, stated, "It is the glory of God to conceal a matter; to search out a matter is the glory of kings." Another way of saying it is: God hid it only to reveal it through the one it is hidden in. Although the above verse mentions that it is the glory of kings to search the matter, God leads the individual king to search, and it is God who brings the matter to light. Apostle Paul, in II Corinthians 4:7, confirms this when he wrote, "But we have this treasure in jars of clay to show that this all-surpassing power is from God and not from us." This means everything is the doing of God when it comes to your origin, destiny, and all that is between.

With God being the One who led you here to read this book, He is ready to reveal this Truth to you. Your heart is searching because you know there has to be more—more to you as a woman, and more for you. You know you cannot continue living an unfulfilled life. For example, you want so badly to get married that you feel like you'll die if you don't walk down the aisle by tomorrow, but what happens after that desire is fulfilled? On the other hand, you prayed to get married, and now you are— praise God—but what next? Your mind cannot seem to comprehend why you still feel empty or not fully there yet. It is almost impossible to "wrap your fingers" around it, but something is just not right. And you know what? It's not, and truly, there is a whole lot more that God is about to reveal to you and through you. This book begins the process for some, while to others, it is a wakeup call to get moving on what He has already announced in the corridors of heaven: your destiny.

In order to get to the root of things, one must dig to the beginning and start the search from there. For if the roots are not dealt with, the surface will be deceiving - as if healed when you are not. Our Heavenly Father is not just concerned with making us look good on the outside; He wants us whole from the inside out. Therefore, for us to get to know who The Woman is, we must begin from where and how she came into existence.

"In the beginning, God created..." This is how Genesis 1:1 reads. God began creation with heaven, earth, light, day, night, trees, etc., and then on to the creation of two very important creatures, popularly known as Adam and Eve. This is what the world has come to know. But, note that not only were they created, they were also made. Moreover, they were in another formation before becoming Adam and Eve. Therefore, when it came to their specific type of creation, two processes occurred in their making. Please keep this point in mind as you read on for better understanding of our core topic, The Woman.

Although there was the creation process, yet another process took place as God created. It was the process of naming creatures, orchestrated by the

Creator. This method did not happen until God made the Man creature, and formed its first appearance as Adam, which played a very crucial part in The Woman's existence.

When God created man, he was simply, yet intricately, male and female, two in one, or better defined, one creature with two different manifestations or prototypes. According to the record found in Genesis 1:26, the Triune God said, "Let us make mankind (MAN) in our image, in our likeness, so that they may rule over the fish in the sea and the birds in the sky, over the livestock and all the wild animals, and over all the creatures that move along the ground." This verse sets the hierarchy of authority within creation, specifically to earthly creatures, but it also reveals the secret of The Woman, which we will get to shortly.

Notice in the above verse that humanity is a type of creation that consists of two distinct forms, which were male and the female. For God said, "Let us make mankind (MAN) in our image, in our likeness, so that they…" (Emphasis mine). Did you catch that? God refers to the making of man as they. Later, in Genesis 1:27, the author wrote, "…God created mankind in His own image, in the image of God He created them; male and female He created them."

In other words, the first creative procedure to make man as creature would result in two different bodies still possessing similar spiritual attributes. Similar in the sense that they both had the same specifications of Creator, origin, imagery, blessing, authority, instructions, and creative transformation.

During this first part of God's divine handiwork, when their bodies were not yet formed, male and female were equal. Why and how were they equal? They were ONE: the one that God created and called Man.

Ah! I can hear all the mental voices of some who are reading this shouting back at me, especially those religious ones, saying, "NO! Male and female are not EQUAL!" But what does that Bible you read really say? In all translations, it is written with clarity in verse 28 that God created MAN both male and female. Note that what was created was MAN, Mankind, or Humanity, and it is a category of creation, put in place to rule upon earth and enjoy the benefits supplied within it.

During this process, there is no distinction between the male and female forms within the Man creature. God made them, gave them their charge, and blessed them both as one. He blessed them as a creature, a product of His creation. Oh, before I forget, He saw what He had done and said it is good. That's right, making them both as one was good according to God's standard. Now, I know it may sound a little confusing to some, but bear with me and I will explain as we go on this beautiful journey of discovering the Strength of The Woman.

So, let's take it step-by-step, or should I say, let's break-it-down. God is at work in the beginning. Seems like He's making everything from heaven to earth, light to darkness, and all that exists within. Then He gets to the point where He wants creatures that resemble and may even function like Him—for the making of Man was the image and likeness of God formed: image relating to God's appearance, attributes or reflections; and likeness meaning behavior, mannerism, character, abilities, and possessions.

Unlike all other creatures, the new creature(s) would have the capability to exist in the spiritual realm, for God is Spirit, and the earthly realm, because they must rule the earth. This new creature must be able to communicate with both Creator and all other aspects of creation. This creature needs power to rule, subdue, and dominate, according to God's charge. This creature should have the ability to be fruitful, reproduce, multiply, and replenish. With all that in mind, God creates Man, a single creature having two dissimilar coverings or outer appearances hidden within. Remember at this point, this creature is created as Man, not in terms of sexuality or gender, but in terms of spiritual conception and being.

Additionally, this creature possessed all the above aptitudes and more! A creature whose only authority is

God. A creature with so much power that it is the reflection of Who God is in earthly form. This new creature is God-formed (Isaiah 43:10)! Wow, I'm getting excited and ahead of myself, so let me slow down.

Now, since God is Spirit, where do you think His mind is? In the Spirit. Also, where do you think three or two can equal one? This right, in the spirit. Therefore, when He said, "Let us make man in our image and our likeness…," it was all in God's Spirit, His very Being, or in the spiritual dimension of creation. Hence, the creation story, as recorded in Genesis 1:26, is all in the Spirit; in the spiritual realm. It was not physical, as we know physicality.

Oh, how I hope you're getting this, and if not yet, hold on, because you will very soon. To explain this further, notice Genesis 2:5 (AMP), where it states "…there was no man to till the ground." But did it not say in the previous chapter that God had created man? So, why was the writer saying that there was no man? If God had made the Man creature, a physical creature, then where did he vanish? If he, or they, were on the scene, why then would the Bible say there was no man? Why wasn't he around to get some work done? That's because he was not yet in physical form and was still in spirit-form as the Man creation, being male and female in one. Furthermore, we know this because tilling or plowing the ground refers to physical work.

This Man creature was simply not on the scene, as were the trees and other kinds of creation. However, when it was time for this Man creature to come into physical existence, God made it happen. Genesis 2:7 records God forming the male (gender) aspect of the Man creature first, which is called Adam. Later, came the female (gender) version of the Man creature, which Adam named Woman. Again, Man in creation-form or spirit-form is both male and female, but gender is not present while in this state because gender relates only to the physical.

This is what happened when it was time for the Man creature to come into physical existence. God shaped dust, breathed the spiritual creation of Man into the nostrils of that dusty form, and it then became a living soul known as a man in terms of gender. In other words, the spiritual components within the Man creature, which was created within the Spirit of God, brought to life the dust formation for physical use on earth. And, what we see first is the male gender appearance or body, which is one aspect of the Man creature in physical form. Up to this point, the female aspect of the Man creature was still in spirit-form, but now existing within Adam, the first physical body.

Due to the limitations of physicality, the dust formation of first man Adam could not display both male and female expressions in one body. That is why, when it comes to gender, one can only be a man or a woman. However, in spiritual form, both male and female can exist as one spiritual creature because gender is not applicable in that realm. Therefore, God's construction of dust brought about a visible separation of the Man creature, making them man and woman in reference to gender. Please tell me you're getting this.

The word 'spirit' (pneuma or ruach) is actually gender-neutral. It mostly refers in meaning to breath or wind. I think one can safely say that there is no gender when it comes to the worlds of spirits. Gender identity relates to earthly things. We only use such forms to describe the mannerism of a spiritual being when applicable. Consider God right here. Is He a male or female God? Is He is Mother or Father? You might say He's Father God. But does that imply that God is man in gender form? No, it does not because God does not live as a physical being. He is God, capable of expressing both characteristics of male and female, because, He is Spirit.

Jesus was once confronted by the Sadducees with something similar to this gender issue, as recorded in Mark 12:18–27. They questioned Him about the resurrection as an event. They inquired about what would take place after resurrection with a certain woman who had seven husbands while alive on earth. Their mean question was, "In the resurrection, when they rise again, which one's wife she will be? For all seven had married her." Well, Jesus, being wise and insightful of their intentions, replied to them appropriately. He first pointed out their lack of understanding of Scriptures, which not only kept them in spiritual darkness, but also withheld the power of God from manifesting in their lives.

Humanly speaking, that sounds like a realistic question, doesn't it? Because really, whose wife will she be in the after-life, knowing the Law stated that due to death, she had to marry each brother. But you see, when it comes to Truth, the carnal understanding of such reasoning cannot produce the answers. Moreover, Truth dwells in the spiritual realm, making it a different ballgame all together from carnal reasoning. For once a person dies or leaves this physical body to enter life after death or the spiritual realm, there is no such thing as gender. Gender identity as male and female, man and woman, or the sexes, comes into existence only through the formation of a physical body and ends once the body dies.

Jesus had to teach them that the resurrection is foremost a spiritual matter. Moreover, I doubt that they knew that the resurrection is a Person and not an event. For Jesus, in another passage of Scripture, declared Himself to be the Resurrection. I bless God that His Spirit is opening our eyes to discern more and more the difference between what is spirit and what is flesh or carnal. Possibilities within the spiritual dimension become limited through the manifestation of the physical. Likewise, things pertaining to the physical do not occur within the spiritual.

Why is this necessary to know? Well, for starters, how will humans reproduce to replenish the earth if Man existed only in the spiritual realm? The Man creature needed both male and female expressions becoming flesh and blood in order to reproduce on earth. In other words, what Man consisted of in the spirit had to be made physical.

That is why God declared that it was not good for man (Adam) to be alone even as He created him. If man now in physical form remained alone, referring to suitability and procreation, he would not have been able to reproduce on his own. He needed a female body to mate with for reproduction. And for that to happen, he had to 'marry' a woman, making her his wife. This is the right way to go about it. It is God's way of replenishing the earth—marriage before baby carriage.

Another thing that Jesus pointed out, when replying the Sadducees in the story of Mark 12, was the reference He made of the angels. That is, He was informing those so-called 'scholars' that angels are spirit-beings with no sex or gender. They are not given in marriage, and neither do they have sex with one another. And let me be straight with you, God purposed sex as an earthly thing only. There is no sexual activity in heaven; and neither is it meant to happen in any other realm between spirits without bodies.

Note that Jesus's reference of the angels gave another important point, which is that they are eternal beings. This means they do not die; they are spirits. Death within the spiritual realm is separation from God. Once this happens, it changes the formation of the creature that is now separated from its Eternal Source of Life. Death in the physical realm is the dying of the physical body, which is already in the state of spiritual death due to the fall.

So, if angels do not die the physical death nor are they given in marriage, could this mean that marriage is only an earthly thing? Is it only for our time here on earth? Might that be a reason why people say, "For better or for worse, till death do us part?" Which death? Surely not the spiritual death, referred to as the separation from God. It must be the physical death of the body. Moreover, if physical death can kill or annul the marriage, then I conclude that marriage is for earthly purposes. But, I'll leave that for another book in this series.

Lastly and very pivotal to our faith, Jesus in Mark 12 revealed something very powerful of the Being of God. I always say that, when we get to know Who God is, we will get to know who we are, since we're supposed to be His image. In revealing God, Jesus helped us to understand something significant about our nature in creation. He stated in verse 27 that God "…is not the God of the dead, but of the living." This blew my mind when I read it this last time.

The God of the living! Christ made mention of Him being the God of Abraham, Isaac, and Jacob. Now, we know these men died, but these proclamations are in present tense. Jesus did not say He was the God of Abraham. No, Jesus quoted from Exodus, "'I am the God of Abraham…'" (Mark 12:26, emphasis mine). Either God died, or Abraham, Isaac, and Jacob continued to live. But we know that God—being Spirit, and the Spirit of Life for that matter—cannot die as long as He's in Spirit form or wears the incorruptible Body, referring to the risen Christ. Although the Patriarchs died in physical form, they continue to live in spirit. God has given us the ability to have the same kind of life as He. This is why He is the God of the living and not the God of the spiritually or physically dead. Now, that's awesome!

He created Man, male and female, with the intention of them living forever. No kind of death was to conquer them as long as they heeded to God's warning and remained in His Source of Life. For God said, "…you must not eat from the tree of the knowledge of good and evil, for when you eat from it you will certainly die" (Genesis 2:17). What God commanded was not meant to exercise dominion over man as some might think of God. No! God was just informing Adam; simply indicating that death was in the tree of the knowledge of good and evil. And if he ate it, the death in the tree would enter into him, because what a person eats spiritually becomes a part of him or her. But no, Adam did not listen and neither did his woman. Then again, what else could have been expected of her, since she was only bone of his bones and flesh of his flesh? She acted like him.

Even after Adam, the first physical expression of the Man creature, sinned and death came in and began to reign in humanity, God still decided to give us eternal life by coming to die for us in the body of Jesus. God's intention for His Man creation never changed. Thus, in spirit, we will and do live forever, especially if in Christ, where there is no partaking of the second death, as Apostle Paul wrote.

Life originated beyond when we first met it in our physical bodies, when we are born or conceived in the womb. It stems back to the beginning and travels throughout all eternity. We can experience it because we are more than simply the gender of man and woman. We were created spirits and will remain spirits, whether we wear the physical bodies or incorruptible ones.

So, who was The Woman in the beginning? Thus far, we have observed that she was the creature God created as the other part of Man, whom He brought to Adam to name. When God said, "Let us make man…" He was creating The Woman, the female part of the Man creature. She was the spirit God gave the charge of rule to when He spoke to them in Genesis chapter one. The Woman was the creature made in God's image and likeness. The Woman is the same as Adam in spirit but with different physical expressions. God revealed him first on earth and her second, but both existed as the same before the making of their physical bodies and the naming process through Adam.

Chapter 3

~ then there was Adam

Some of you may be wonder why I chose this chapter heading, "Then There Was Adam." I did so because we are concentrating on The Woman, and what surrounded her or influenced her existence both spiritually and physically is important. It is also significant that we know that she is a part of the Man creature. In Truth, she is the Man creature. However, immediately after the time she reaches full earthly manifestation, her formation changes from that of a male structure to a feminine body. Remember that she was in Adam as spirit before coming into the physical female body.

Whilst in spirit, or as the Man creature, all she knew was the Creator and herself as to what God spoke when creating them in Genesis 1:26. I believe she knew who she was, for in Him we know all things by the working of His Spirit. However, after her formation as human, she lacked in understanding of what God had said and what He did not say. In my opinion, it was Adam's responsibility as head and *namer* to update her.

The Woman was the second appearance of the Man creature, and Adam, by divine design, was first. When I speak of appearance, I am referring to the visible image seen in the physical state of things as they were, prior to the fall. The *Fall* is the occurrence of the 'original' sin entering into God's creation allowing death to reign. Also, note that what we see as our environment today is in a death state. Could this be why the search for the Garden on this present earth is futile to some?

No one has been able to pinpoint the exact location of the Garden with infallible proof. Yes, there are rivers with the same names as those written in Genesis chapter two, but it has not been proven that the Garden of Eden is where these rivers begin. So, when one is studying the Creation story, it is imperative that he or she sees it through the eyes of the Spirit, and not with human analogy only.

Adam was the first of their (male and female) kind in creation to walk the earth, and the first to interact with other aspects of creation. Adam was also the first to have a conversation with God. There is no record conversation between The Woman and God prior to the naming process in Genesis 2:22. Now, if there was one, I wish had included the facts about the trees of the Garden before hearing whatever she heard, or did not hear from Adam. Sometimes the message changes or loses its effect when communicated from a second party to a third; not received from the source directly.

Anyhow, being that Adam was first to manifest, when God formed her body and brought it to life, she was faced with Adam. Actually, she was presented to Adam. After meeting him, she began to receive from him. She fed from him and her existence from then onward depended on him. Mind you, Adam named her and she was from that point what Adam called her. For he said in Genesis 2:23, "This is now bone of my bones and flesh of my flesh; she shall be called 'woman,' for she was taken out of man."

It is fascinating that the Bible uses the word 'now' in the declaration made by Adam. In other words, from henceforth— meaning forget what you were, because all of that changes from now on. The Woman is now the product of the physical man, Adam, who had become the authority after God Almighty. The Woman, who is now Adam's woman, has come into submission of this hierarchy.

You see, when God deals with humans, especially when it comes to visions mainly destiny, He finds one person and makes him or her the head. Yes, many could be involved with the vision, but it is to only one person God gives the vision. When God wanted to start an earthly nation of covenanted people, He found and chose Abraham and made him the Father of Israel and the Father of Faith. When God wanted the spiritual nation of kings and priests, He raised up Yeshua, Jesus the Christ. Likewise, when He needed the human race on earth, He brought Adam out first. By the way, this in no way limits a woman from being chosen to head anything, even though I only gave examples of men who were used. I do humbly say that when God wanted I Am Precious International Ministries to begin, He called me, a woman.

God works with humanity where it is, eventually raising it from that state of darkness to levels of light. After He released earth to Man, God left the responsibility and the accountability to them; Adam being first to appear took charge. It was at this point that the imperfect set in. Let me articulate that God was perfect in His way by making and empowering a creature to have supremacy on earth. God gave Man authority and trusted that their decisions would be as good as they viewed and/or desired it. But how many of us have come to realize that our views are sometimes shortsighted, blurred, or overrated?

God could have named all His creation Himself, but that would have frustrated the whole purpose of creating and making this Man creature. In addition, how then would have God been able to manifest Himself to His creation since He was Spirit? He had to release the authorization to rule and the naming process was the first part of that function. Adam did what was expected as the first human. The Woman had not yet arrived and when she did, everything created had received its name except her.

God demonstrated true leadership, something Adam needed to really learn and practice. The Creator reproduced Himself as an image, and gave His production the ability to exercise rule, authority, and choice. But what did Adam do? He, unlike His Creator, confined the woman to himself. And what I main by this is that there was no responsibility given her beyond Adam. Her identity was to be his helpmeet. After she was named, The Woman became Adam's by flesh and bone. What happened to the creative formation God spoke concerning her in Genesis 1:26? Why didn't Adam declare that over her when naming her?

All she reach was to Adam, to the extent that nothing she did was impactful until it had reached Adam, be it good or evil. Not even the eating of the tree of the knowledge of good or evil was eventful in itself until Adam ate of it. Whether she spoke to the serpent, trees, or water, none of it was significant because only Adam was the prime authority. He did not breathe out of himself her spiritual capabilities as part of her name when he first named her. All of that remained in him. Thus, she had lost her value and equality as the female version of the Man creature. And, if one argues that she didn't, then my question is, why didn't sin have an effect when she ate of the tree?

Unlike God being her only authority when created as the Man creature, Adam now becomes her direct head because she is in human form. The Scriptures do not state that God breathe into her dust-formation like He did in the case of Adam. Since this was not so and there was no need for it, I conclude that she depended on Adam to breathe into her what God had breathed into him concerning her as equal part of the Man creature. Unfortunately, Adam named her, and that name description set a cap on who she became in manifestation, which hindered her spiritual realities. Oh, the limitations of flesh.

Then there was Adam, an authority that could not take responsibility for the actions of those under his care, and neither could he take responsibility for his very own actions. As I'm writing this, I'm really seeing the inequality in the Garden of Eden. They were no longer equal after Adam encountered The Woman, which I strongly believe was not God's intention and I'll prove with Scripture as we go along. However, I do believe that they were one in some actions on earth.

Again, the Man creature, male and female, were one. When the Man creature became visible as Adam, he made The Woman God brought to him different from what she was purposed to be. Through his naming of her, she became his woman and no longer The Woman. Even though, he and The Woman had the same origin, flesh had brought in the great divide, spiritual inequality, identity crises, and gender suppression. A deeply rooted problem that only Christ, The Word, could bring union to. This divide has brought so much discomfort to women, most believe as they are growing up that only a man can soothe their aches and bring life to their essence. Thank God, He is delivering His daughters from such mental bondage and spiritual stagnation.

I can hear you now: So, Precious, are you saying that it's wrong to desire the comforts of a man? No, that is not what I am saying. I am asserting that, once you come to discover who The Woman in you really is, you will look to another source as Strength and Comfort. You will begin to see the man in your life, or the one God will bring you to as husband, the way God intended it. That man will then be a resource, and not the Source of your life.

Now you may ask, "But isn't that how it's supposed to be? Am I not supposed to submit and be under my husband and seek comfort from him and direction, etc.?" Yes, you are, but with the understanding of the whole picture of who you are to him and in God. My purpose is to bring spiritual wholeness to women, so let me make it plain. Adam was not the source of The Woman; he only limited and distorted her views in consciousness of who she was. It is this inaccurate view that has crippled the spiritual realities of The Woman and has brought her under much enemy assaults as Adam's woman or now Eve. And do you know that some men still behave as the first Adam instead of the Last Adam, who is Jesus? Oh yes, they do.

Until now, both men and women have blamed God for being the One who initiated this format as such: women are subservient to men. It is not true, and God did not do it. This misconception and demonic mindset is due to the misinterpretations of the statement God made in Genesis 3:16 when He said, "…Your desire will be for your husband, and he will rule over you." Distinctively, this was after the fall of Adam and his woman, and God was only describing whom Adam's woman was, which was what Adam named her in the first place: bone of my bones and flesh of my flesh. What else was she to manifest, desire towards God, the Spirit? No! Since Adam named her, she was to manifest what he called her bone and flesh. This, my friend, is the power of the naming process in creative form, and God respected the authority He had given to

Adam, regardless of the consequences of Adam's human actions.

While God's intention was to have a helpmate for Adam, one who could rule, subdue, and dominate with him, Adam changed things. For the Creator said in Genesis 2:18, "It is not good for the man to be alone. I will make a helper suitable for him." I believe this helper was to manifest all that was spoken of her in Genesis 1:26. Her strength should have been that of God, because her intended responsibilities required it. Frankly, her capabilities were to match that of the Man creature in the physical. Now I'm not referring to bodily strength; I'm relating this to the authority she was to carry. But isn't it thought-provoking how our realities can turn out different from God's intentions for us until He steps in with mercy on our behalf? Hallelujah!

The Strength of The Woman is coming alive in us more and more in Christ. Unfortunately, when this strength surfaces, some men are afraid of such women or intimidated by The Woman who exercises this dominance given to her by the Creator. Some consider this unruly, rebellious, and insubordinate behavior, or may even relate it to the spirit of Jezebel. Well, I'm not referring to women who have no regard or submission to authority. Nor am I praising those who are outside of the acceptance of God's grace and feel that they are just as equal with men. That carnal mindset is wrong.

On the contrary, I speak of The Woman who is exercising the authority God gives to her, being led by His Spirit. This kind of manifestation, again to some men, is too powerful and out of the norm of what they are used to, since no human can control or dominate The Woman. This Woman knows from whence cometh her Strength, regardless of flesh and bone.

Although the flesh made the divide, I recognize that it also set in place authority. But this kind of authority, of the man being the head of the woman, relates to marriage and the context thereof. No man is the head of a single woman besides her earthly father (biological or via honor), or a spiritual head, which could be male or female by gender. Furthermore, I acknowledge the headship of the first Adam over all women in relation to the human race, and that of the second and last Adam, Jesus Christ, as it relates to His Headship over all that exist. The single woman has Christ as Lord if she submits to Him, and should never feel incomplete because she has no earthly husband. Her spiritual covering is Christ, her Head.

God will use a woman, and a man, when it comes to manifesting His Presence and carrying out His Will. Mary, the mother of Jesus, is a prime example to help illustrate my point. We see Mary, a teenage virgin, completely taken over by the Creator. In the Gospel of Luke, chapter one, the writer tells the story of the birth of Jesus and states how Mary became pregnant. Obviously, God decided to use an unmarried woman, a virgin. God could have waited until Mary and Joseph married and then withheld Joseph from having sexual intercourse with her since He did not need a man's sperm? Yet, He did not. His Holy Spirit overshadowed Mary and she was found with child prior to marriage; all done supernaturally.

So what am I saying? I'm saying that you, as a single woman, do not have to wait for a husband before you move on with your life. God can use you to the fullest, and you can find your identity in Him regardless of your marital status. And when you do get married, hey, He will continue to use you as He sees fit.

Yes, God had Mary get married immediately after the conception, but that was to protect the child and her life due to the pressures of society, traditions, and religion. Joseph further played significant roles in the life of Jesus as an earthly father, and the life of Mary as a husband. Still, Mary's source was God when it came to the holy child she carried.

God grants us the grace for wonderful marriages, but He is the Source of your strength, Woman. And even though Joseph came in the picture, Mary still had to look to God to get her through the sufferings she bore as the mother of Jesus, especially during his death. Society, I'm certain, still ridiculed her for her "bastard" child. Even now, if one does not get deliverance from the strongholds and dictates of society and family pressure about this marriage issue, that woman could end up destroyed emotionally. Please note, I am not saying go and have a child outside of marriage, and nor am I saying don't get married. Certainly not. But wait on God, and change your mind about how you view your life without a man as husband while you wait. God is your Strength.

Marriage is wonderful and a God-given gift to humanity. In my physical form, I am single as I wrote this book, but I am not alone or incomplete. I look forward to my marriage and definitely anticipate seeing the man God has for me, but I'm not delaying my life because I'm not yet married. Neither am I killing myself emotionally due to the absence of an Adam. God forbid, I do not sit in depression because it has not manifested yet. I know The Woman inside of me.

Saints, the enemy—for years—has stifled the fruition of women in all dimensions, especially when not married. So many fall victim to the serpent's condemnation and lies of the absence of an Adam. I wish I could hammer it in that the earthly Adam is not your Source of life.

Yes, he is the source of the misconception of who The Woman turned out to be in the Garden, but he is not the source of who you can be in spirit. The enemy has used this as poison, spitted out all through the world. For years, many have positioned the daughters of Eve as second-class citizen. In fact, the place of women in some societies was and remains to be the home and nowhere else. Many women were restricted and confined to the bedroom, kitchen, and the children. Outside of that, they have no existence. They have no choice even when it comes to whom they married. Seen as merely a sexual instrument of lustful pleasure to quite a number of men, women are taken advantage of and disregarded. Sadly, such beliefs and malpractices continue to this day.

One story in the Bible makes me laugh when it comes to mind. It is the story of a woman caught in the act of adultery, found in John 8:1–11. The focus of the story was to trap Jesus in His interpretation of the Law and His decision on how to apply the Law, which would have resulted in the judgment of that woman. Here's how it goes:

Jesus returned to the Mount of Olives, but early the next morning he was back again at the Temple. A crowd soon gathered, and He sat down and taught them. As He was speaking, the teachers of religious law and the Pharisees brought a woman who had been caught in the act of adultery. They put her in front of the crowd. "Teacher," they said to Jesus, "this woman was caught in the act of adultery. The Law of Moses says to stone her. What do you say?" They were trying to trap Him into saying something they could use against Him, but Jesus stooped down and wrote in the dust with His finger. They kept demanding an answer, so he stood up again and said, "All right, but let the one who has never sinned throw the first stone!" Then he stooped down again and wrote in the dust. When the accusers heard this, they slipped away one by one, beginning with the oldest, until only Jesus was left in the middle of the crowd with the woman. Then Jesus stood up again and said to the woman, "Where are your accusers? Didn't even one of them condemn you?" "No, Lord," she said. And Jesus said, "Neither do I. Go and sin no more."

WOW, is what I say!

We can glean so much from this passage. But the funny thing is: where was the man? I have never heard of a woman caught in the act of adultery alone. There must have been a man somewhere in the act with her: and if so, where was he? Why wasn't he also brought to Jesus? The Law of Moses in Leviticus 20:10 says, "If a man commits adultery with another man's wife—with the wife of his neighbor—both the adulterer and the adulteress are to be put to death." Okay, maybe she was unmarried and that's why they brought her alone. But even so, she still could not have acted alone.

Society stood ready to stone that woman to death. Adam was ready to limit her to nothing. But, this was not so with the Last Adam, Jesus Christ, Who was now on the scene. Instead, He wrote in the dust. If I were to analyze this, I would say that He was demonstrating similarities to what He did as God the Creator in the Garden of Eden when He created The Woman: You were asleep, Adam, during her creative process. How dare you condemn her or put her under? It was God who wrote on the dust His Word to bring the Man creature into physical existence. God Who breathed His life in the body, making it a living soul, and all of a sudden, and the Adamic nature wants to take life. How daring!

Unfortunately, this attitude and death-like nature traveled into the church age to the point that scholars interpreted Apostle Paul's statement in I Timothy 2:12 to mean women should not preach or take high authoritative positions in the church. A woman was not to exercise rule over a man. Preposterous! Reading 1 Timothy 2:12–15 (NASB), Paul wrote:

Likewise, I want women to adorn themselves with proper clothing, modestly and discreetly, not with braided hair and gold or pearls or costly garments, but rather by means of good works, as is proper for women making a claim to godliness. A woman must quietly receive instruction with entire submissiveness. But I do not allow a woman to teach or exercise authority over a man, but to remain quiet. For it was Adam who was first created, and then Eve. And it was not Adam who was deceived, but the woman being deceived, fell into transgression. But women will be preserved through the bearing of children if they continue in faith and love

41 | SOTW

and sanctity with self-restraint.

And may I add II Corinthians 14:34–35 that says, "Women should remain silent in the churches. They are not allowed to speak, but must be in submission, as the law says. If they desire to learn anything, let them ask their own husbands at home; for it   is improper for a woman to speak in church...." That alone makes me want to be quiet. But humorously speaking, who do I ask if I am still single?

If Apostle Paul's message should be interpreted as we read it, why then does he say in I Corinthians 11:5, "But every woman who prays or prophesies with her head uncovered dishonors her head—it is the same as having her head shaved." We are aware that prophesying is a Gift of the Holy Spirit for the edification of the Church. We do not prophesy to ourselves under this unction, for the Gift comes into manifestation in a gathering of the Body or two or more members.

So whom exactly was Paul referring to in this verse? If women, then why is it these women could speak publicly and the others in the Corinth church were to be quiet? Or, is it that the Holy Spirit's gifting to women is for prophecy only and not for teaching? I believe that, somewhere along the road, issues concerning women were wrongly interpreted or some men just enjoyed continuing the practice of keeping women under the Law. Whereby, Grace has set us free.

One thing is certain: it is the Holy Spirit Who gives the ability, and it is also Him Who permits us to function in Him. I have come to the understanding that God is not blind, and neither is He confused about gender. He knows a man from a woman. If women are not to walk in the operations of the Spirit's gifting and callings when it comes to the building of the Body, then He would not gift women and neither would He call them to positions of authority. So, since He does, it is time for the Body of Christ to uproot this highly satanic mindset from our midst and allow God to use His vessels—male and female—as He sees fit.

We are no longer under the Law of Moses, but under the Law of God's Spirit, which is freedom in Christ Jesus. The Law of the Spirit gives life, the life that delivers from all forms of death and darkness. What women were not to do under Law, they are now free to do under Grace in accordance with the Life of the Spirit. Mind you, The Woman of the Church is a new creation from The Woman in the Garden, Adam's Woman and Eve.

Before touching on any of that however, let us consider the relationship between Jesus and Mary Magdalene. She was a sinner delivered from demonic possession through the power of Christ. Mary made Jesus her Lord and Master, and this was before He got on the cross to die, resurrect, ascend, and glorify. Her love for Him was deep and rich, drawing from a well of appreciation. Had it not been for Jesus, she would have been killed, for the Law would have sentenced her to death.

Mary was trapped in the woman Adam named. There was no opening or access to the creature she was created to be until Jesus came and presented to her the power to overcome in and through His Blood. This former sinner met the Second and Last Adam, the Adam that placed a name on her and changed her nature and position in life forever. No longer was she bound to the dictates of the flesh and bone scenario. He made her free to live in the Spirit of Life and the Spirit of Creation.

Perhaps, Mary Magdalene became conscious of where she was from as the Man creature, because she sure did live after her encounter with Christ as though she knew where she was going. We see Mary in John 20:17 cleaving to her Lord at the tomb. The separation was unbearable for her. Three days probably seemed like three centuries with Jesus dead and buried. Suddenly, she recognized Him when He called her by name.

Imagine her expression of joy, which flooded her heart and eyes with light and life again. His pronouncement of her name, Mary, did not resemble the sound it made when mentioned by the other men before Christ. He brought her alive. He gave her hope and acceptance. This Adam was different from the ones

44 |

she had prostituted with, the ones who prostituted her, and the ones that did not consider her marriageable. This Adam gave her a reason to make her want to never let go of Him. She held to Him not as a physical companion or boyfriend because He was not that to her, but as her Source of Life.

Now concerning the Church, it was Mary who Christ instructed to go the other disciples. She served as an evangelist, the first one after the resurrection. Jesus could have appeared to the men without her help, but He decided to do it this way. She did not recognize Him at first and probably thought he was a worker of the tomb or a gardener like Adam. Which means that He had to reveal Himself to her and He did not have to. Yet, He did.

God is revealing Himself to His Body and His Body is Spirit, not flesh and bone. The Body of Christ, the Church, may have the identity of the female, but it is not within the context of gender or sexual organs. God will use any spirit He chooses, despite the covering of gender upon the spirit. We need to focus more on the spiritual aspects of our existence as created beings, and not see the things of God from a one-dimensional view of carnality.

The Church must continue to frown upon the gender issue within it. Segregation of women and men in local church gatherings should no longer be among us. Using the words of the writer of Hebrews, I will say, "Let's move on from these elementary things and grow in the Spirit" (Hebrews 6:1-2, paraphrased). As long as an individual receives the Holy Spirit's baptism, that person has all rights to function through the leading of the Spirit when it comes to ministration with order and great discernment.

Something I need to point out from I Timothy 2:12 is the meaning of the word "authority" or "rule," depending on the translation. The King James Version records it like this: "But I suffer not a woman to teach, nor to usurp authority over the man, but to be in silence." Apostle Paul was absolutely correct by stating that a woman should not usurp authority over the man if said in context of the relationship seen in the Garden of Eden. Indeed, even if said according to the creation of the Man creature. God's idea was not to have the genders usurping authority over each other. No. He intended that they collaborate and work cohesively as one. Thus, any woman trying to dominate or control a man is wrong and vice versa. The man's authority over the woman is by virtue of which came into physical existence first, nothing else. And even that authority has its limits and boundaries.

Jesus is the First of the brethren raised from the dead. I quote Colossians 1:18, "And he is the head of the body, the church; he is the beginning and the firstborn from among the dead, so that in everything he might have the supremacy." That positions Him as first and the One that exercises the authority associated with being First. However, we do not see Christ dominating those that are His. He deals with us in love and equality. His desire is that we know the Father and have the Life of the Father.

We know that we will never be first and we dare not think of such. But hypothetically speaking, what if someone did covet that supremacy? It would be a waste of time because that Seat is occupied and it will never be vacant. Not only that, we have all that we need just where He placed us, in Him seated at the right hand of the Father. Is there any place better? Moreover, when one sees it through the eyes of the Spirit, we are in the highest position for we are in Him and He is in us. We are One with and in God. There is no higher place to covet. Glory be to God.

Christ does not suffer from insecurities. There is so much to God, and in God, that sharing Him provides all of what each person needs abundantly. I'll share this revelation with you that Father God gave me some time ago. In the Book of Psalms, we hear King David say often, "The Lord is my portion." This acknowledgement is also mentioned in other parts of the Bible as well. Now when one defines the word "portion," it means a part of a whole; an amount, section, or piece of something.

So, literally, if I were to state this, I would say the Lord is my portion or I have a piece of God. The only problem with this is the Truth that God is One and cannot be divided or split up into pieces and portions. If I take a piece of pie, I have reduced it. But when it comes to God, He cannot be reduced, which means that He is not a portion as we may consider portions.

Father God told me that whoever has Him as their portion has All of who He is, and not a piece of Him or a portion of Him. Do you see why it is vital we see things from the spiritual dimension? Each one of God's children has a portion of Him, and that portion is actually All of Him. I love that!

The Woman has the portion of God. She has all of God because Christ, the Last Adam, has named her and given her His identity, which is her true identity. Come out of the old, dead, Adamic state and mindset and enter the New where there is no identity crises or inequalities. Christ's naming process is exactly as the Creator for He is the Creator, and this time, He is not passing you on to some self-centered sucker. No, this time, He is bringing you to Himself, where you have always belonged.

Then There Was Adam. Which Adam? Because we sure don't need the one old…

Chapter 4

~ here comes the snake

This chapter will explore the story of Adam's woman and the serpent, which commences in Genesis 3:1. What do you think is the Truth behind it? Did it really transpire the way we were told in Sunday school? Does it resemble the pictures we see, with the partially naked woman in a garden scene and a snake dangling from a tree and the appealing red apple? Was there a conversation between that woman and snake? Do snakes talk?

Now on a serious note, this is how one should

probe for Truth. Examine all things from all angles known. The Bible in 1 John 4:1 says, "Dear friends, do not believe every spirit, but test the spirits to see whether they are from God, because many false prophets have gone out into the world." That is, many false messengers and messages have gone out into the world. Test, test, test, and test again. Discern—ask the Holy Spirit—research—probe—question—and ask the Holy Spirit again. Whatever it takes, get to know the Truth, for the Truth you come to know will set you free.

The Garden of Eden was the paradise of Man. It had everything both male and female needed for survival. A preacher once said, and I paraphrase, "The woman met all she needed upon her arrival. Adam lacked something, which was her, but she had it all." Listening, I thought that was the end of it, but my mind is changing as to whether or not The Woman did have it all, or rather, got it all.

When God formed her, Adam was asleep. Figuratively speaking, he was oblivious to her making. Some things are better kept secret, wouldn't you say? There was no interference from him or any other creature. Her making was between her and her Creator, and she did have it all when she arrived on the scene. The only problem thereafter was her subjection to the authority of Adam once she met him and received his name.

It was a problem not because of submission issues,

50 | SOTW

but because of identity concerns resulting from the naming process. You see, when Adam named The Woman "bone of my bones and flesh of my flesh," she was subjected to the physical realm of flesh and bone transforming her to Adam's woman. The spiritual aspects were no longer her primal identity. She became more conscious of her physical nature rather than the spiritual. As time went by, she lost her clarity of the Voice of God and His Word because her mind related more with the lower nature of what she now was, Adam, instead of all God.

The name Adam "is both the proper name of the first human and a designation for humankind. The color red lies behind the Hebrew root adam. This may reflect the red soil from which he was made. Adam was formed from the ground (Gen 2:7). Word play between 'Adam' and 'ground' (adama [h'm'd}a]) is unmistakable. It is important that Adam is identified with humankind rather than any particular nationality." (Taken from BibleStudyTools.com).

The Woman—coming from a bone (rib) of Adam, receiving the name, Woman—means that this Woman was all-human in an unfallen state of sin and death. Her spiritual state was locked up somewhere within Adam, the first man by gender. When he named her the first time, he did not bring into manifestation her spiritual capacity or nature. Being totally of the earth and earthly, she related and interacted with things of the earth, including the serpent, which from beginning she had dominion over; however, she could not exercise it.

The serpent was not a snake as we see reptiles today. It was not a long, belly-crawling creature that most will not dare come near or have any interaction with. One must examine the Creation story in a parabolic way. Look at the symbols in the story and receive interruptions from the Holy Spirit of what they reveal of spiritual realities. So, if the serpent was not a physical snake, as we know it today, then what was it and what does it represent for our understanding?

When the Bible speaks of the serpent, or what we call the serpentine spirit, it refers to the subtle, crafty, deceptive, and destructive nature of the spirit at work. Because the serpent has beautiful and shining skin, it is able to appear attractive and innocent, not projecting its poisonous venom. It delivers lies and half-truths. In other words, when this spirit speaks through thoughts and impressions within one's mind, it takes the lie and conceals it in some form of truth, making it believable. This spirit is able to appeal to the senses of man and has a way of convincing its hearers, especially if they do not know the whole truth or believe in the Truth.

Genesis 3:1 describes it having a beast-like nature yet its appearance is shiny as a serpent. However, it is important to note that God created it this way and brought it to Adam to name it. Thus, Adam, and I suppose his woman, were aware of the nature of this creature, particularly Adam who named it to be what it was. In the beginning of creation, it is a serpent, but when we read of it in the Book of Revelation, it is the dragon, that old serpent. This is because it has grown big from feeding on the flesh (dust) of man.

The serpent in Genesis is familiar with the order set forth in creation, ideally, the man being first and the woman second. It did not engage in conversation with Adam but rather with his woman. Meaning, it did not break rank or the hierarchy of things. It probably figured out that Adam would not give in to its nature of craftiness, because Adam had within him the nature of deity. However, the woman was the nature of Adam, bone and flesh. You see, this spirit lingers, watching for an opportune time to make its move. It perfects its skills by studying its prey to see where the weaknesses lie, and when the opportunity exists, it begins to slither towards the identified prey. This, I believe, is what occurred in the Garden between this spirit and Adam's woman.

The woman's physical senses were alert. Genesis 3:6 describes her appetite for the fruit as she looked at it. In addition, her comprehension of what was good for self was intriguing. In fact, this woman of the Garden, who Adam named, submitted so well to authority that she ate and gave some of the fruit to him. So, when it comes to authority and submission, the woman had it down pat within her making. The serpent observed this aspect of the woman and knew that, if it could not get to Adam, it could get to him through his woman. The deception worked within the scope of authority and submission.

Another feature of The Woman was the possibility to exercise authority over the man. Remember, God gave them both authority, and, although it was shut up in Adam, the chance of it being activated in his woman existed. Could that be a reason why Apostle Paul warned about women (wives) usurping authority over men (husbands), if that was the meaning of his writing? This, I am convinced, was in reference to a man and his wife, and not to women in general. Anyhow, it is true that, when someone receives warning not to do a thing, it means that the individual can do what he or she is being warned against. That is what happened in the Garden, with God warning of the tree of the knowledge of good and evil. He knew that the possibility of Adam eating of the tree existed; thus, He alerted him not to.

Adam, as well as his woman, could not handle the power behind that particular tree. Have you heard the saying, "Knowledge is power"? Well, it is. It is powerful because things of the mind like thoughts, knowledge, imaginations, dreams, etc., are spiritual in nature. Each thought a person thinks carries a spirit with it. To be precise, thoughts are birthed from the spiritual, which could be from the source of a human spirit, demonic spirit, angelic spirit, or the Holy Spirit.

Thoughts are messages, signals transmitted to and within the mind. The spirit behind the thought is what makes it powerful, and neither Adam nor his woman could control or dominate the spirit of the knowledge of good and evil at that time.

For starters, it was foreign to both of them now that they were in human form, especially his woman. If a human cannot control a spirit, the spirit will influence and control that human as a host. We see an example of this mentioned in 1 Corinthians 14:32 when Paul wrote, "The spirits of prophets are subject to the control of prophets." As believers, we are instructed to be led and controlled by the Holy Spirit of God. Our human spirits must submit to Him if we claim to be born of Him.

In the conversation between the serpent and Adam's woman, the serpent said, "For God knows that when you eat from it your eyes will be opened, and you will be like God, knowing good and evil"(Genesis 3:5). Thus, she concluded that eating of the tree would make her wise, based on what the serpent said to her. We then extract from this statement that there was a power within the fruit of that tree, and Adam's woman discerned it. However, could she handle what she discerned and now desired?

Evil was present in the Garden of Eden. That's right! Evil was present, but its power was not activated within the realm of humanity. Up until that point, evil existed within the realm of knowledge coinciding with good, and not within the human realm. You might be wondering, How can evil be present in what God made? Well, does it not say in Isaiah 45:7 (KJV), "I form the light, and create darkness: I make peace, and create evil: I the LORD do all these things." So there we have it: evil was created and it existed in the Creation story of Genesis because He made it so. However, it laid dormant. God said, "Let there be light..." permitting it to exit and have its effect as light did. He never said let there be evil.

The releasing of its power happened when Adam ate of the fruit that evil and good were planted in. I am reminded of the statement Jesus made in Matthew 7:16 when He said, "By their fruit you will recognize them." In other words, by looking at a person's actions, you will get to know his or her nature, or the spirit that is in control, through how it influences thoughts and actions. When it comes to trees, we can know the nature of them by what they produce, because the nature is in the seed within the fruit.

After God had finished His work of creation, the only person that could release evil was Adam. He did so when he ate and became aware of it. He granted permission for spirits to exist and manifest in the earth because God had given Man the authority over earth. Adam's eating of the tree allowed that nature to come into manifestation, because evil is a spirit and spirits need human vessels to operate in the earth. Eating then implies the direct or indirect acceptance of a spirit within a person's life, and the granting of permission for it to manifest.

We are to eat the Word of God or the Bread of Life, Christ Jesus. When we partake of Him, He comes alive in our lives and we begin to manifest the nature and character of His Spirit. On the other hand, if we spend time watching pornography, for example, we fill ourselves with the spirit of lust and eventually will display sexually immoral actions. These are spiritual illustrations with physical descriptions. Thus, when we look at the couple eating the fruit of the tree of the knowledge of good and evil, we now understand that it was a spiritual act with physical connotations to explain what took place in the Garden. God does use physical things at times to reveal the spiritual dimension, so that we gain better understanding of the unseen world in order to subdue it and exercise our dominion over it.

How can one subdue what he or she does not know or has come in contact with? How could Man, both male and female, have dominion in the earth if Man did not have an experience with everything in the earth? Or, why would God say subdue when there was nothing to subdue? But mind you, there was, and Adam and his woman encountered what needed to be subdued when they ate of the tree of the knowledge

57 |

of good and evil. Unfortunately, they did not have the power to dominate the forces evil brought with it, including sin, hell, and death.

I have heard preachers blame the woman for the fall, speaking of Adam's woman present in Genesis chapter three. Some would say, "If the woman had been close to her husband, she would not have been talking to a snake." Or, "It was the woman who disobeyed God." On the other hand, "She was weak so she fell prey." Now that I think of it, is she really to blame or is this another Adamic trick to suppress The Woman and not be responsible for self-actions?

When one is confined to a certain place, he or she has no choice but to function within the limitations of that setting. He or she becomes subjected to the bounds and properties set therein. One parable says, "Where you tie the goat that is where the goat will eat." Well, The Woman was no different. She functioned within the confinements of who Adam named her to be. Nonetheless, something happened.

Her first nature of the female aspect of the Man creature kicked in. That is, the creature God made in His Spirit cried out for expression. Adam's woman wanted to be like God, the Creator. It proved that that there was more to who she was, and that part of her was tired of being tied up and held hostage behind the scenes.

No matter how long one keeps a dog in a house, it is still a dog. It can never be human, despite how many tricks it learns, beds it sleeps on, or food it eats. The true nature of what it is will always surface. Now that is extreme, but it shines light on my point. God made The Woman, yet He also created her. She had a spiritual formation as well as a physical one.

Although the physical became first- nature by the time she met Adam, the spiritual was there somewhere, in isolation or obscurity, and when the serpent-like creature spoke with Adam's woman, it triggered the god-like nature buried within her; engrained in the cells of bone and flesh. This began her search for her true identity and destiny.

Even though it started through the message of a crafty creature, Adam's woman realized that something was missing, yet needed, because she desired it. If you do not need or want a thing, you will never desire it. Desire springs from the need of a person, which points out the lack or absence of that thing. The individual may or may not be aware of the lack, but through situations, conditions, and circumstances, that void will surface, becoming recognizable to the person in question. If the woman did not feel the need or absence of wisdom in knowing good and evil, she would not have desired it. Moreover, if she did not desire the need to be like God, she would not have desire to eat the fruit, no matter how pleasant it looked.

Her temptation in the Garden was due to her lack, birthing her desire to fill that void. Something is never a temptation to someone if she or he does not first want it. The reason we use the word "temptation" when we face certain situations is because we desire that thing so badly, yet we know that we cannot or should not have it, either at that moment, at all, or by such means. So, what the serpent does is to present what is lacking to the person through a means that is either illegal or immoral. And based on the strength of the desire present within the individual, he or she will either give in to the temptation or let it go.

The woman desired to be like God, and her desire led to the presentation of the temptation. Could it be that the Creator somehow orchestrated the whole episode between Adam's woman and the serpent? And, if He did, was it because Adam had failed to reveal her true identity to her as The Woman? The Bible says in James 1:13–14, "When tempted, no one should say, 'God is tempting me.' For God cannot be tempted by evil, nor does he tempt anyone; but each person is tempted when they are dragged away by their own evil desire and enticed." Thus, we understand that God did not tempt this woman, but the temptation came through the serpent due to her desires. What God did was allow it all to happen to bring out what was hidden in her.

Why was she uncertain of what God had said?

60 |

What prompted that desire of wanting to be like God? It seems as though Adam's woman knew she lacked in some areas of her life, precisely, in the areas of wisdom and divinity. Although he named her bone of my bones and flesh of my flesh, his bone and flesh was not sufficient for her, and neither was it able to make her like God. She wanted more, and so did he. But, they got into it the wrong way due to their wrong motives.

She wanted wisdom and divinity; so, what was wrong with wanting what seemed good? Could she have been lacking what was already there? The Book of Proverbs discloses that Wisdom was there in the very beginning of God's creation. In fact, Jesus Christ is the Wisdom spoken of, as He is also The Beginning. James 1:5 further states, "If any of you lacks wisdom, you should ask God, who gives generously to all without finding fault, and it will be given to you." Now do you see where the problem was? She and Adam looked to the wrong source.

Moreover, to be like God is to possess the nature of divinity, which the woman lacked now that she was subject to flesh and bone. So what was she missing? Or rather, Who was this woman missing, that brought her to the realization of her needs? Listen here ladies, Adam was just not enough, and I believe God permitted the craftiness of the serpent-like nature of that beastly creature to bring to her attention the possibilities of who she could be...because that was who she really was.

Are women suffering in this present life because they lack the True Knowledge and Nature of who they are? I believe so. Adam did not do well in the Garden, and God the Creator would not stand by and allow His creation to experience such deprivation without providing a remedy. If you follow the story outlined in Genesis chapter 3, you will see that God releases the divine capability of Adam's woman as He addresses the serpent in verse 15 saying, "… I will put enmity between you and the woman, and between your offspring and hers; he will crush your head, and you will strike his heel." Remarkably, "God is not a man that He should lie; neither is He the son of man that he should repent…" (Numbers 23:19, KJV).

What He purposed from the Beginning and in the Beginning, that is, in Christ, He will ensure happens, for His Word cannot return unto Him void, according to Isaiah 55:11. His intention was to have Man, the creature with both male and female expressions, exercise dominion as God on the earth. So, who said that it is only the male gender? Again, in Christ, Who is the Beginning, there is neither male nor female, as we know gender (Galatians 3:28).

Getting back to the serpent, we see that it played, and continues to play, a very significant role in the lives of humans. It is there as the spirit that mirrors what our physical and spiritual natures desire, whether one is a believer or not. Looking around the world today, humans desires either to be like God or to be a god. In some way or the other, these beings have the propensity to strive for greatness and some will use any means possible to arrive at the peak. Unfortunately, the means by which the serpent presents the desired thing is not of God, nor does it fall within the perimeters of how God's Word states desires should be attained.

One day, while the Holy Spirit was teaching me about temptation and desire, I   asked Him a question. I wanted to know the difference between Adam's woman in the Garden, wanting to be like Him, and me with my similar desires. Wasn't it the same desire expressed? Why was hers not good and mine acceptable or pleasurable to Him? For a little moment, as I thought about it, I felt like I was being like Adam and his woman in the Garden and almost resentful of my desire. Well, within moments, the Holy Spirit corrected and comforted me by pointing out the difference.

You see, if God is not the One leading a person to Him or making that person want to be like Him, then it is evil in nature. No human can make himself or herself like God, no matter how much knowledge they acquire of the realms of good and/or evil. In fact, God makes it clear in I Corinthians 3:19 that the wisdom of this world is foolishness to Him. How much more foolish is the knowledge that is wrapped in craftiness as the serpent spits it out?

God is Wisdom and He is the One who makes us wise. He is the Sole-Proprietor of divinity and gives it as He wills. Every other means is ungodly and falls short of His standards of perfection. Thus, Adam's woman looking up to a tree to make her wise and make her like God was abominable. Moreover, that lower creature presenting it to her made it even worse.

We are to submit upward and not downward. The Woman had become so lost in what Adam made her that she opened herself to the lesser realm of the animal kingdom to receive and feed from it.

How can something that is below you give you instructions or insights about what is higher? The serpent had not experienced the higher realms. The serpent was not like God, so why did she not discern the means through which the temptation came? Apparently, in the Kingdom of God, the lower does not give instructions to the higher. God does not communicate to the lower in rank to instruct the higher. It does not work that way, and if God uses such means, then that individual was not listening and was disobedient to Him in the first place.

There are quite a few examples of this, and I recall Numbers 22 illustrating one incident of it through the story of Balaam and the donkey. Balaam did not heed the Voice of God when God spoke to Him the first time. He was so stubborn that God had to get the donkey to speak to him and bring correction.

In as much as that was not the case of Adam's woman, we still can gather that, if we do not get to know what God said about us from His Word, another source will try to convince us otherwise. Adam's woman was enticed by the serpent, but if she knew who she really was, that whole conversation would have ended differently.

We can see a similar scenario of this in the life of Jesus and His encounter with the same old serpent as found in the Gospels. Like I said earlier, the serpent will present to us possibilities to achieve and satisfy our desires but we have to decide whether to yield or not. Jesus had desires, great dreams flowing all through Him during those forty days of fasting and prayers. He needed to eat, wanted to be known as the Son of God, and desired to have full ownership and authority of creation as the Image of God, Man.

Can we say those desires were wrong? No, they were not, because that was whom He was and what He was sent to accomplish. However, He was certain not to give into any other means of achieving those goals apart from the way God had marked out for Him. Unlike the first Adam and his woman, Jesus knew that His Father in Heaven could fulfill all that He desired. Christ also knew who He was and did not have to prove anything to anyone.

Jesus also understood the promptings of His fleshly nature and did not allow it to dictate His actions, for He was a man under control of the Holy Spirit. Jesus identified more with His divine nature than His human nature and He lived His life as such, even unto death. He already knew He was God, although He was subjected to the limitations of His flesh and bones. So, what did He do? He waited on God and did not yield to the tempting of the evil and crafty serpent in order to fulfill and satisfy His needs.

Another point that we can relate to is the Truth that Christ was God from the Beginning. Stripped of all His divine nature, Jesus walked the earth as 100% man. This relates to our examination of The Woman because, to some extent, Adam denied her of her divine nature when he named her. But unlike Jesus, she and Adam settled with the serpent and ate of the tree. Christ did not.

Holy Spirit gave this key to me when I asked Him about the difference between Adam's woman and myself when it comes to desiring to be like Him. He taught me that as long as it is God Who is leading me and giving me desires, it is not a problem at all, because He will fulfill them. But if it is through other means and for wrongful intentions... I best watch out for a possible fall!

On that note, I would like to ask you to examine where you are when it comes to your conversations with the serpent. Are you yielding to his promptings to temptations or are you waiting for God to do it in and for you? If you desire to be like God, note that it is ONLY God who can make you into His Image and Likeness. And since that is a God-given desire, allow Him to do it His way and in His time.

Note that the serpent-like spirit will only exercise dominion over you when you yield to its suggestions of how to satisfy your desires. If those desires are lustful in nature, then be aware that the serpent already has a place in you. Our desires are to be pure and holy. For example, if you are a married woman desiring your husband, then that desire is pure and in the right context of God's Word for marriage. On the other hand, if you are a married woman desiring or lusting for another man apart from your husband, or   for another woman, well, you already know what that is and which spirit is in control there, because it is surely not the Holy Spirit.

As I conclude this chapter, it is needful to emphasize the fact that the serpent, or the tempter, will seize the opportunity to reflect to you what your desires are, be it good or evil. When you recognize the need at that point, examine if it is lustful or divine. That is, see if it is a desire placed there by God or of your own accord.

Once you have concluded which it is, rule out the lust and hold on to the God-given desire. As you do, discern the means by which you think you are trying to fulfill that desire. Is it in God's timing and in His Way of doing things?

Do not be like the children of Noah, who tried to build the Tower of Babel in Genesis 11:1–9. They were united, which was a good point. They even had a good intention in building. But what exactly were they trying to accomplish that God had to end?

Check yourself to be sure you are not trying to build a name for yourself in your attempts to build God's Kingdom, because that desire is not of God. Watch for the subtle snake-like nature wrapped in some form of Truth. Christ is the One building His Church and Kingdom, and it is only His Name that is exalted, not yours or mine. We must be mindful not to give any room to the devil by being ignorant to his devices, as the Apostle Paul alerts us in II Corinthians 2:11. This I speak mainly to saints both in the Church sector and in the marketplace.

Chapter 5

~ where was God

To answer this chapter's question, I will say that God was where He is, and where He will always be: Everywhere. He has not moved and has not changed in anyway whatsoever. However, the best place to search for God is to look for Him in Spirit. Jesus, in His conversation with the Samaritan woman about worship's best location, found in John 4:24, said, "God is spirit, and his worshipers must worship in the Spirit and in truth." Being in Spirit is always the best place to find God.

A reader might be concerned now as to whether God goes missing at times. King David, in the Book of Psalms, tells us that God hides Himself in darkness; or rather, He makes darkness His covering. Moreover, none of us humans has the capability of seeing clearly in the dark. If so, how then will we see God since He hides Himself?

In order to see God, He would have to give the individual access to His realm. He reveals Himself to His creation when He chooses. Being Spirit, the natural will never see Him, unless He manifests Himself in some form or the other. Being the Holy Spirit, the spiritual man in a fallen state of sin also will not see God, because His holiness keeps all forms of sinful darkness away. God is God and no one can reach Him except He initiates, approves and leads the search.

Therefore, where was God during the episode in the Garden of Eden? I tell you, He was right there in Spirit. Precisely in our take on Adam's woman, it is safe to say that perhaps she questioned where God was during the encounter with the serpent. She was posed with a question from it about what God said, so I assume she immediately tried to focus on where God was. Is not that the first question that crosses the mind when something goes wrong, or when an issue arises, that has some link with God?

If you are anything like Adam, you probably do what he did, which was to blame God in the aftermath.

And I'm hoping you're not. For people are very quick in blaming God for conditions that turn for the worst. I too have been guilty of shifting blame on God for not keeping me from sin when I did not exercise my dominion over it. Yes, I know we say, "It was the devil," but somewhere in our minds, we question ourselves, or even God directly, as to where He was and why did He allow it to happen. A famous question is, "Why does God allow bad things to happen to good people? He's in control and can stop evil," and on and on and on. This is a natural Adamic response, but what should be the right way of inquiring God's take on what goes wrong in our lives?

One should be mindful that this type of attitude and conditioning of the mind can produce a silent anger and resentment towards the Maker. Often, people become angry due to their unfortunate situations, and that anger in the heart keeps them in bondage to those spirits. I remember a very clear incident of this in my life during my teenage years. I hoped and prayed for my life to go according to my good planning. All I wanted was to remain a virgin until marriage, have and raise my kids, and simply be a good Christian woman.

I trusted God to keep me and work it all out for me this way. After all, it was a small thing for Him to do. Darkly, my life went in a totally opposite direction. I'm sharing this with you for your deliverance, if needed, as you further see the craftiness of the serpent. Before reaching 18 years of age, I was drugged and raped. It was not a violent rape, because my whole body was under the influence of the drugs. But I felt the violence deep in my heart when I realized the next morning that I had lost my virginity. It felt like a big sword was thrust in my whole being and I wailed out a cry that never audibly sounded. I felt my world come to an end, because my dream of being a virgin bride had ended.

What did I do as I silently grieved? I asked God, "Why?" The pain was deep and all I knew was that I was finished. Yes, I was a believer and very strong one, who was having holy visitations and encounters with the Heavenly realm. Jesus was my Best Friend and we walked together, so my trust in Him for my dream was easy to develop, until that very worst night of my life.

Although I had strayed a little from His path, I thought I could handle it and continued to encourage that 'so-called' boyfriend. I was also trying to be like my schoolmates. I figured that it was innocent by nature and I had made myself clear to him on the issue of sex. Even more, I still trusted God and believed that He was going to answer my prayers. Well, I was blinded and ignorant of the devil's devices at that time.

However, once the virginity state was gone, my only prayer thereafter was, "Lord, why couldn't you do this very simply thing for me? I didn't ask for gold, money, and all other materials things; I asked to be a good Christian." How hard was that?

I traveled with the disappointment for years. I was learning to recondition my mind without realizing the spirits of darkness held my heart. As I went through life, be it in the Church setting or in the world's system, since I was becoming a very good backslider, I thought my love for Jesus was as it was before. Yet it was not, because my heart was embedded with dirt and openings for demonic interactions.

So, where was God in all that? He was right there, watching, loving, and preparing for my deliverance at the right time. I did know the condition of my heart towards God. For the heart is dense and deep, capable of all evils. It was not till one day, when I went to another man of God's house, that deliverance began for me in the course of our conversation. God was ready to set me free, and it was my time to begin the healing process. I saw it all before my eyes; hurt, anger, resentment, disappointment, lack of trust, etc. I held them towards my Heavenly Father, and yielded to His deliverance. Boy, was it a process to freedom.

After being set free, I still held on to areas of my life by building a wall around my heart. One area in particular I refused to surrender to God until He was ready again to help rescue me. It's funny how we think we have it all figured out when we cannot even see all that is hidden in our hearts, minds, and spirits. It takes the Holy Spirit of God to search us out and bring to surface what is and is not of Him.

Now, looking back, being completely free and surrendered to my Heavenly Father, I regret why I was angry with Him. But it's okay now, because I am in the Father and the Father is in me. No more do I wonder where God is or question His Presence in life. I know where He is and can see Him always. I hope my sharing of this testimony is of help to you or someone you know.

All of our knowledge of God traces to the beginning, and in that faraway place or time, He was there. Genesis 1:1 starts with the description of Creation, introducing us to the Creator, God. The very first time we hear of God, He was doing something, and it was something good. Based on the track record I know of Him, He does not change. Thus, if we ever wonder where God was or is, we should relax and know that He is doing something good everywhere He is.

The woman, I believe, began to have a third- party relationship with God after she met Adam. Prior, it was she and God, but once He handed her over, it was she and Adam. I determine this by her not being able to fully know what God said concerning the tree of the Gardens. In Genesis 2:15–17, when God first spoke of that tree, the woman was not yet in created human form. She was bottled up in Adam. Only Adam's physical ears heard the knowledge and instructions about the trees. The woman received God's word through Adam, and we know that communication can alter when passing through various channels.

On the other hand, the serpent was somewhere around or at least in the Garden when God gave that word to Adam. The woman, speaking of gender, was the last unveiling of God's creation process in the Garden that we know of. Every other creature was already there, including the serpent. It must have gathered its information from a source in order to question the woman. Unfortunately, Adam's woman did not have all the facts right. Or, was she blinded by the void she felt that caused her not to take the time to assess all the words of the serpent? Notice the conversation from Genesis 3:1–5:

> And he said to the woman, "Indeed, has God said, 'You shall not eat from any tree of the garden'?" The woman said to the serpent, "From the fruit of the trees of the garden we may eat; but from the fruit of the tree which is in the middle of the garden, God has said, 'You shall not eat from it or touch it, or you will die.'" The serpent said to the woman, 'You surely will not die!' For God knows that in the day you eat from it your eyes will be opened and you will be like God, knowing good and evil."

First of all, she should have detected the stupidity of the serpent's question. If God had said not to eat of any tree, where were they eating from all along? Duh!

Secondly, was she not aware of the trees in the midst of the Garden because it was more than one tree there? Genesis 2:9 tells us that in the midst of the Garden were the tree of life and the tree of the knowledge of good and evil. However, she only made mention of the tree of the knowledge of good and evil being in the midst of the Garden.

Adam's woman truly needed to know God for herself. Her knowledge of her surroundings as passed down from Adam was not precise at all. God will trust other individuals to give us the knowledge received from Him, but it has to be as He said it. Many in the religious system of mystery Babylon (found in the Book of Revelation, and what we call 'the religious church') preach and teach things that are contradictory to God's Word. They minister fables, lies, deception, bondage and the whole nine yards of demonic messages. We have come to believe in stories that have blinded our eyes from seeing the Truth of God's Word, which have hindered our relationship with the Father.

These lies are now strongholds in the minds of many believers, and they are unable to experience spiritual growth in their lives. Take, for example, the devil that believers know as Lucifer. Where is the Truth and what is the lie in what we have learned about this take on Lucifer?

- Point #1 – Lucifer is not a name, and neither is it the name of the devil or some fallen archangel. Bible studies prove that only the King James Version uses the word Lucifer. Almost all other Bible translations have stopped using it, or never used it at all.

- Point #2 – Since Lucifer is not his name, then there was no angel that fell from Heaven with the name Lucifer that some claim is the Devil. Which means, the whole story of this rebellion in Heaven by this supposed Lucifer never occurred, and the serpent of Genesis 3:1 is the real devil.

- Point #3 – We see the word Lucifer mentioned only once in the Bible and it's in Isaiah 14:12, which means "day star" or "morning star."

Well, we know that the Daystar or Bright and Morning Star is Jesus our Lord. So, how can the devil carry such a title or name if the meaning of Lucifer refers to Jesus?

Should we dare to go further with this, we will see that the reference of Lucifer spiritually spoke of Adam, the first man, and not the devil. Only Adam was made as the reflection of God's glory to all of creation. Only Adam brought in the light that came from God, for God is Light. This whole story of it being the devil who was a worship leader in Heaven and rebelled is off. We as believers must begin to search the Scriptures and not believe everything we hear, no matter from whom we hear it. I will leave it at that, and pray Holy Spirit brings revelation of this to you because it will produce great levels of freedom, and I encourage you to conduct your own research for the Truth of His Word. It's about time each person knows God for him- or herself. We cannot afford to live like Adam's woman.

Now, where is God in all this? Well, He's bringing Truth in manifestation to His creation, because Truth has already come in the Person of Jesus Christ. He said in John 14:6, "I am the way and the truth and the life." In your search for Truth, you may ask, Why did God allow all this to happen? Well, Man—both male and female expressions—need to subdue as a part of their makeup and destiny. Hence, one can only subdue what is chaotic and disorderly after he or she learns how to subdue.

It is all written in the Creation story, but it takes the eyes of the Holy Spirit to see the hidden treasures in His Word. The fall took place right there, when the war started with man and beast. The beastly nature wanted to rule Man in human form, instead of the God-given divinity they already had. It was the fight between the head, Adam, representing the fullness of man, versus the serpent, which represented what was unruly. God had no part to play in that fight, except to watch it all unfold, as He already knew it would. Now it was time for Adam and his woman to know what to do and learn how to live God's way.

God, being omniscient had already, slain the sacrifice that would redeem man from their fallen state. For the Bible says in Revelation 13:8 that Christ is "...the Lamb slain before the foundation of the world." Let me stop here to give some encouragement as you go through what may seem like the attacks of the devil or the hard times of life. Every problem has a solution in God, and Christ has paid the price for you to receive your answers and breakthrough. Though it appears long-suffering and never-ending, be patient for the pieces are unfolding according to plan. Your victory will be great and nothing will hinder it from happening in your life. I prophesy an ever-increasing grace to you in every area of your life, and that the victory Christ won on the cross for you will manifest according to God's divine timing. It is bound to happen in Jesus's Name.

You see, the battle was never with some angel trying to overthrow God and take over His Throne. NO! It was not at all. God is just too Great for such nonsense, and people need to stop believing the enemy's twisted information, which are lies, and reach into God for His Truth. Evil has always been the force trying to overcome good and God made it that way. But Man can overcome and destroy every form of evil as He did in the person of Christ, God's Last Adam.

It was the first Adam who wanted to be like God.

In fact, it was his woman who actually made the statement of wanting to be like God. On another dimension, the female represents the soul, Adam represents the spirit, and the Garden their body: the soul being the mind, with all its faculties, expressed the desire to be like God. This being said, all of man as a creature was in accordance with the woman's statement.

Adam, being the head and given to the eating of the tree, was responsible for her actions, for he was intertwined in her. Moreover, his participation in the act disclosed that he too desired to be like God. However, we do not know what the density of the matter was nor the state of man's heart until God revealed it in Isaiah 14:12-13 and Ezekiel 28:2. It was man all along who wanted to ascend into the Heavens and be like the Most High. It was Adam, not forgetting his woman, which ruled next in line to God from the very beginning. My proof of this is visible in the ascension of Jesus Christ, the Second and Last Adam, after His death, burial, and resurrection. That place of authority belonged to Adam, but the first Adam lusted and sought for ascension his way and not God's way. The Last Adam, Christ, did receive His ascension and glorification God's Way.

God had given the authority and position to the creation called Man, not the serpent. There was no war between some stupid serpent or an angel and God. The warfare is and has always been between man, along with his woman, and the serpent with all that it represents. The devil desires to rule man, not overtake God. The devil took the place of God in man's life when man, both male and female by gender, granted it permission in the Garden by heeding to its seduction. Once the first human rendered obedience to the other voice, it became lord over all of humanity. The voice of the beastly nature that sprang up within man's hearing and his obedience to that nature subjected him along with everything under him to the new lordship of the devil or the evil one.

Dear reader, in the beginning, the serpent was powerless over Man. The power given by God was directed to Man, which brought everything else under Man's control, or at least it should have been. The enemy only gets power when we submit to him by heeding its suggestions and believing its lies. Why? Because, in our obedience to the spirit trying to influence us for control, we relinquish our power to that spirit. But again, the Creator set the record straight.

The story continues to unfold where God steps on the scene. In Genesis 3:8 (KJV) the Bible states, "And they heard the voice of the LORD God walking in the garden in the cool of the day: and Adam and his wife hid themselves from the presence of the LORD God amongst the trees of the garden." Before moving on, I don't know if you detected that the voice of God was walking. To me, that's amazing. How can a voice walk? Other translations say the sound of God walking etc., but the King James Version of it just knocks me out.

So, the Voice of God is now walking but walking where? In the minds or hearts of Adam and his woman, and they are the only ones at that point to have changed. The serpent remained the same for a while, but God was the same consistently.

Notice that the first action of the humans was hiding. Now come on, how can you hide from the One who is Omnipresent? Read what King David wrote about hiding from God in Psalm 139:7–12: Where can I go from your Spirit? Where can I flee from your presence? If I go up to the heavens, you are there; if I make my bed in the depths, you are there. If I rise on the wings of the dawn, if I settle on the far side of the sea, even there your hand will guide me; your right hand will hold me fast. If I say, "Surely the darkness will hide me and the light become night around me," even the darkness will not be dark to you; the night will shine like the day, for darkness is as light to you.

I love it, love it, love it, and I love it. The beauty and soothing words in this Psalm is breathtaking with Truth spelled all through it. Too bad David was not there to write those lines for Adam and then play them out for Adam with his harp. Notwithstanding, hiding is another first-nature response of man when he or she sins. For some reason, you know you're in trouble, so you take off for covering. LOL

I remember how the enemy used this weapon against me for years in my early adult stage, which of course was after the incident I wrote about earlier. I was still a believer and loved the Lord wholeheartedly, or so I alleged. But I still had a problem with the sinful nature, and thought I needed to make myself holy. I did not have the Truth of God's Word, embedded and active in me, that stated that Christ is my Righteousness and He had made me holy. In my mind, my actions and outerwear determined my standards of holiness per day. I had even gone to the extent of burning my short skirts and other provocative clothing, thinking that it would make this holiness issued settle in me once for all.

Apparently, it made me feel good, for it had a form of godliness to it, but unfortunately, it did not root out the cords of the Adamic nature in my heart. It is one thing to know of something but it is another to live out what you claim you know. What the enemy did concerning this area of weakness was to make me feel extremely guilty for sinning, to the point that I would run away from God instead of running to Him. My life went from one extreme to the other immediately after I had sinned.

In that state of mind, my conscience condemned

me more than I could bear, and what was worse was that I got too ashamed to return to God for forgiveness. The result of feeling guilty led me to avoiding God and everything that had to do with Him. It sometimes felt like I was on a long roller- coaster ride, with one moment on fire for God and the next backslidden beyond the gates of hell. It grew into a pattern, creating cycles in my life to the point that my friends and others did not take me seriously when I professed my Christianity.

But praise God, He knew how to handle that spiritual bondage in my life, and since that faithful day many years ago, I have never left my Father's Presence. Now, if I sin, which I don't consciously do like before thanks to Grace, I straightaway launch to Father for forgiveness. On the other hand, I release assaults on any and every demon lurking around. My friends, we can live a sinless life. Not by our strength but by His Spirit. Don't settle for the lie that no one is perfect and so you conduct your life in a manner unworthy of the King's child. No, otherwise God would not have said "be holy for I Am Holy" (I Peter 1:16, ESV). If He said it, then it is so.

God had to teach me that my sin was between me and Him and no other spirit or person. He was my appropriation for sin, He paid the price, and He made me holy. My sin no longer can make me unholy, for holiness is a positioning in Him and nothing can separate me from that. What I don't do is live a sinful life because I no longer can. I am now a slave to righteousness. In other words, righteousness is my Lord and Master. My obedience is to God, and through my thoughts and actions, I've given Him the authorization to control and lead me. I believe that is how it should be in your life, and I encourage you, just in case you haven't received that strength yet, to yield fully to God.

He is forever calling unto you, Woman, as He did in the beginning. He is asking, "Where are you, woman?" Where is the Woman God made, and not the one Adam named? What happened to the female God called out in the beginning and gave authority to according to Genesis 1:26? I believe she is somewhere hidden in you, and the real you is coming alive as He is shedding light from this book. This is an intimate moment between you and your Maker. He is the One who brings a person out of darkness and places him or her in His marvelous Light (I Peter 2:9). Jesus is saying, "Come." So, stop reading, take this moment, and talk to Him with the words He's putting on your heart.

Okay, you are back. I hope you had a lovely time in communion with the Lover of your soul. Now, we can continue with this book, "Strength of The Woman: Her Making."

During the interaction after Adam's woman had

eaten of the tree, you will notice that she says nothing until addressed by God. And, perhaps, she would have said nothing if Adam had not shifted blame. Can you imagine, a woman remaining quiet? Now, that would have been a miracle.

Interestingly, she does exactly what Adam did, shifts blame to the lesser, except that Adam indirectly blamed God, his Higher. Adam's woman was just like him, when they both should have been just like God. What would have happened if his woman had simply admitted that she wanted to be like God? Would there have been a need for justification from her? In a believer's walk, he or she must learn that surrendering to God is a must-have attitude. But let me draw your attention to what Adam said about the woman.

In Genesis 3:12 (KJV), Adam said, "...The woman whom thou gavest to be with me, she gave me of the tree, and I did eat." Did you catch that? He knew that the woman was given to him. The Woman was a gift and not a trophy! He did not win her in a male chauvinistic competition. Why then do some men feel that a woman is their personal property to do with her as they please? She was a precious gift from the Creator to him, a helpmate, to be accurate. When a man decides to marry a woman, he must realize that she is becoming God's gift to him and not a slave he just paid for. I reiterate, The Woman was a gift and Adam had nothing to do with her formation or God's decision in granting her to him. Adam did not create her, and neither did he know how she arrived on the scene; therefore, he did not own her. To him, she was a gift, and to God, she was His image and likeness.

To God, The Woman was a helper to rule and have dominion alongside Adam on earth. There was meant to be gender equality, which was to be passed down through the generations. But, why is it that we find many women regarded as second-class citizens in quite a number of places on earth? It is from Genesis chapter 3 that we hear folks say, "It was God who delivered the woman to such a state." Still, let's look at what God said to Adam's woman, since this chapter focuses on the role God played in being present, or, perhaps, in His alleged absence. Genesis 3:16 reads, "To the woman he said, 'I will make your pains in childbearing very severe; with painful labor you will give birth to children. Your desire will be for your husband, and he will rule over you.'"

Ah, there we have it: God brought the woman under subjection to the man, or should we say to her husband. But did He really? If you observe from the time of Adam's naming of her, her desire was already for her husband, and Adam already ruled over her. God only spelled it out in black and white. It is like someone wanting to say something but does not really get it out. Instead, he or she goes around to dodge the main point, but not with God. God just said what it was, and redirected her back to Adam, since her desire was seemingly turning in the direction of wanting to be like God, which led her to lust for the tree of the knowledge of good and evil because of what she thought could be gained from eating of it.

What God did was to increase her labor pain and suffering, and it sure has, so I've heard. Moreover, if God is to multiply her sorrow and pain that means that she already had sorrow and pain somewhere in her. He was not giving her something new. Not at all. He was increasing what she already possessed as Adam's woman. Hence, the question is, how did she have sorrow and pain while in the Garden of Eden? What were the causes of such emotions? Was she not perfect when God formed her physical form? Indeed, she was. So, then, where did it all come from? It derived from the name she received from Adam.

God did what He had to do, which was to let it all fall apart in order to put it right. Adam had messed things up from the beginning in terms of The Woman. God allowed him to make his errors, which were his learning curves. The Bible, referring to Jesus, says in Hebrews 5:8 (NASB), "Although He was a Son, He learned obedience from the things which He suffered." Adam's case, along with his woman's, was no different. Obedience is learned through suffering, brought on by the flesh. Do you see this happening in your life? Learning obedience is hard but very possible, especially, if you are quick to obey.

So, where was God? Well, getting deeper, I will say, God buried Himself in the vessels of dirt and allowed the dirt to die in order to manifest. Children of God, as Apostle Paul says in Romans 8:18, "I consider that our present sufferings are not worth comparing with the glory that will be revealed in us." You may say that Paul spoke after the fall, but we need to realize that, the moment God wrapped Himself in dirt, which was the formation of Adam, it was a fall waiting to manifest. And it did began with the bodily expression of the female aspect of man.

God trusted women and had no problem giving the first Woman over to Adam. God knew what she was made of, a secret that has been hidden for years. Every time man, a husband, society, tradition, the enemy, or whatever else, pushed her down further, God was raising her back up. The way upwards in the Kingdom is down. And now, God is bringing out Himself in manifestation of The Woman.

Be on the lookout for your revealing!

Chapter 6

~ *my Strength as Woman*

With all that you have read or probably heard, if you attended the Strength of The Woman Conference, you will know that there is more to a woman as gender than what meets the eye. She is more than beauty, fine apparel, expensive jewelry, pampered treatments, and all other things women do to look and feel their best. A woman is more than a successful professional, a respectful wife, a loving mother, and a trusted friend.

She comprises of all of the above and more.

Adam's woman was not only the one to birth the seed that destroyed the serpent, but she was also the one who became "the mother of all the living" (Genesis 3:20). I found it interesting when God opened my eyes to see that Adam named The Woman twice. The first time, she was bone of his bones and flesh of his flesh. In the second naming process, she became, Eve, the mother of all the living. Why rename her in the first place? I would have thought that the first name should have covered everything, but obviously, it did not.

Genesis 3:20 records Adam calling his wife Eve. Most likely, her name meant living. What woke him up? This name should have been the first; instead of a mere description of what he wanted her to be, simply, woman. God did not just call him man, but named him as Adam. Was it to be different in the case of The Woman?

There is so much in a name. Thus, I alert you, Daughter of spiritual Mount Zion that you should never answer to a description that is not you. You have a peculiar name, and your name should represent what your destiny is to look like. Finally, The Woman not only receives another name and nature, she receives a destiny. The Woman, turned Adam's woman has become Eve, and she now has something worth living for, which is to produce all the living. That only problem with that is, she is to produce the living in a spiritual dead state because of the fallen position they find themselves due to the eating of the wrong tree. In other words, everything she produced thereafter was spiritually dead or separated from God.

Notwithstanding, I believe that God had something vital to do with this change in Adam's mindset and view of the woman. Adam realized that he ushered in death through his actions, so someone had to bring life back. It is no surprise to me that hundreds of years later, God kept Joseph out of the way as He overshadowed Mary during the conception of Jesus Christ. Only a woman could accommodate God coming into earth in human form to deliver life back to it. And this blessing has been like a curse to The Woman, or so it seemed.

However, God knew and trusted that she could handle it. He trusted in the making of His Woman. He formed her in the secret place, away from all eyes, and it is in this secret place that He brings His Woman to the world. Once in Christ, we are no longer a man's property, Adam's woman nor Eve. We are changed to God's Woman, the better version of the female He spoke into being in the very Beginning. Yes, a married woman is for her husband but that is within the scope of earthly things, and, as we discussed earlier, marriage is for the earth. When it comes to the Spirit and the spiritual where Christ dwells, The Woman belongs to God and God alone!!!

No one is permitted to take God's place in her life

for He is always there to protect her. She no longer seeks ways outside of God's doing in order to be like Him. This Woman knows that she is like God as first-nature, and this is not something she is becoming. It is already sealed and settled in God, and when He presents her to the Last Adam, she is All that He is and All that she can ever be.

The Woman has a Strength that is far beyond human reasoning, religious dogmas, and knowledge abilities. Her Strength is not in human physicality, for there is no need for that in the Kingdom of God. Her Strength is not found in gender equality as some seek nowadays, and neither is it in human recognition and rewards equal to that of a man. There is no competition as to who is stronger when defining this Strength. It is in a class and realm all by itself, and it is only reserved for the female version of the Man creature born of the Spirit of God.

"The Lord is my Strength," says a verse we quote often (Psalm 28:7) and a prayer we pray, but what does it entail? The Woman now needs God like never before. The ages are coming to an end and time is running out. This God-like manifestation needs expression to all of creation as God is in Heaven. It is not a mental conditioning, a mind-over-matter strategy, nor some do-it-yourself process. To bring God's Woman out, it will take God and His working alone.

When this Woman begins to emerge, she will require The Strength of a God-Man. Do not for a second think that this is some distant revelation that relates to the Church as Christ's Bride. It does, to some extent, and I will write about it in the series to follow. But for now, it speaks to you as an individual. Are you the expression of the Father in earthly manifestation of Who He is in Heaven?

I am referring to living your life now from Eternity down into time. These mysterious acts as I earlier mentioned are of the Lord's doing and require the Lord alone as Strength. The Strength of The Woman is God Himself. In this dimension of relationship, there is no in-between or middleman, as we saw in the case of Adam and his wife. Yes, this Woman does belong to someone, but that someone is God in the form of Christ Jesus.

The Apostle Paul teaches in Colossians 2:8–10, "See to it that no one takes you captive through philosophy and empty deception, according to the tradition of men, according to the elementary principles of the world, rather than according to Christ. For in Him all the fullness of Deity dwells in bodily form, and in Him you have been made complete, and He is the Head over all rule and authority…" Christ is the embodiment of All that God is. The Woman is highly blessed to have Him as the Man in her life.

No more does she need to look to another or

search to fill a void, because there is no void. And when I speak, please be sure to know that I refer to the spirit called 'The Woman', and not necessarily Eve with her earthly needs.

As for This Woman, God satisfies her and meets her every spiritual need, which greatly affects her soul and body. There is no evil temptation to try to beguile her into thinking she needs to be like Him, for she is Him. She that is joined to the Lord is ONE Spirit with Him (I Corinthians 6:17).

Might I interject here that this new Woman is beyond Eve. This new Woman, who belongs to God, is not away somewhere in this life, taking suggestions from the serpent. Absolutely not, because she keeps the serpent under her feet by the authority she holds in God. Furthermore, she is seated with her Lord and Master in Heavenly places, subduing all other powers and principalities.

I admit, women have gone through a whole lot, and it was all worthwhile. The lesser The Woman went in human form, including her emotions and deadness of spirit, the higher she rises in divinity through the saving Blood of Jesus. This is another mystery of the Godhead. Everything changed when Christ Jesus arrived on the scene of creation in the land of Israel over 2000 years ago. His Presence and work over every imperfection, reconciled all back to God, including The Woman.

As we explore higher revelations of who this Woman is in the series to come, we will experience The Strength allotted to her being. The Strength of The Woman is the Lord God Almighty, and there is no separation or dividing wall between her and His Spirit. They are One. Who she was in the Beginning in the Person of Jesus Christ is who she will be eternally in Jesus Christ.

The Woman is you, and I declare by the Hand of God that you no longer answer to any other name or description that does not coincide with Who God named you. All it takes is one breath from Him, and you will become the Living Soul of God on Earth as He is in Heaven, with all Love and Grace, Power and Might, Strength and Dominion, Forever and Ever.

Amen.

PERSONAL NOTES

THE AUTHOR

Olivia Precious Cooper is the President of I Am Precious International Ministries and G'Strat Foundation, Inc. She's called as an Apostle and Prophet of God. As part of her assignment, she provides mentoring to current and potential leaders. She is a philanthropist, author, and psalmist. Precious ministers to bring God's Word forth with Anointing for understanding and daily application. Christ uses her to awakening His body by unlocking destinies, imparting mantles, delivering and developing those called into ministry within His Kingdom. She presents her life as a conduit through which Holy Spirit creates spiritual transformation in attitudes and atmospheres by prophetic prayers, worship and utterances. She travels extensively, reaching God's people throughout the world. Apostle Precious was born in Monrovia, Liberia, and currently resides in the United States of America. Although, she is totally committed to the work of ministry, her greatest passion is to know God as she is known by Him.

Resources

I AM Precious International Harvest Ministries
Sunday Glory Service
Thursday Mentoring Sessions
Friday Night Prayer 9pm central time
For access: Dial +1(218)632-0947 pin 2010#

IAP Publishing is a branch of I Am Precious International Ministries creating Godly changes in attitudes and atmospheres.

Website: **www.preciousinternational.org**

Phone: +1(615) 669-6460

Books

The Invisible Image: *God's Makeover of the Heart*

Kissed And Killed: *You too can rise from the grave of betrayal*

Precious Living Words *(Parts 1 & 2)*

Hannah Prayed: *And Changed Destiny*

Order your copies today @
www.preciousinternational.org

www.ingramcontent.com/pod-product-compliance
Lightning Source LLC
Chambersburg PA
CBHW060806110426
42739CB00032BA/3111